IN DULCI JUBILO

Poems and Prayers for Christmas
by
Mary Fleeson

GW00361176

In a borrowed room He took His first breath
of warm straw-scented air.
Not for Him a luxury palace,
with perfumed breeze and opulent style.

In a manger He lay, He slept, and cried
and wriggled His toes.
Not for Him a gold-leafed crib,
unique, ornate, and lovingly carved.

On a night like any other night
He changed the world completely.
Not for Him a high-born birth
with a voice of power already-made.

On our day of rejoicing
let us remember that baby boy,
so humbly born,
and be His voice today.

Never mind the hype,
the tinsel and the fairy lights.
Never mind the Santas
or the calorific bites,

Never mind the silly songs
or the really, really sad ones.
Never mind the corny films
or the endless re-runs.

Never mind you've heard it all,
every reading and benediction.
Never mind you've seen it all,
every painful contradiction.

Never mind the hype,
the hollow holiday style.
Only mind the love
in that tiny baby's smile.

Creator God, May Your light shine wider
than the sparkling lights and flickering
candles, help me to bring Your light
to others this Christmas.

DO you know the King
who didn't have a golden crown?

Do you know the Man
who spoke of love and mercy?

Do you know the Son
who shared his heavenly Father?

Do you know the Child
who challenged temple leaders?

Do you know the Baby
who breathed,
and changed the world?

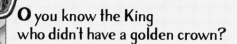

King Jesus, I am here,
on my knees,
Brother Jesus, I am listening,
speak to me,
Saviour Jesus, I am grateful,
thank You.
Radical Jesus, I am Yours,
send me,
Baby Jesus, I need You,
change my heart.

Undulating hills, star-lit and peaceful,
Gentle baa-ing from a lamb,
Night birds calling, 'All is well!'
Shepherds mumbling softly,
Sharing stories, telling tales.

Then.

Oh so bright! Angels above!
Oh so loud! Angels singing!
The sheep, terrified, scatter hither and thither.
The shepherds, terrified,
fall to their quivering knees.

'Do not be afraid!' the angel said.
'I bring good news!' the angel said.
'Great joy!' the angel said.
'Why us?' a shepherd dared to murmur.
'Why me?' I echo his timid words.

The good news is ours today as it was then.
Come with me to the Christ-child.
Fall to your quivering knees
and look upon the face of God.

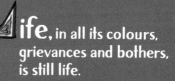

Life, in all its colours,
grievances and bothers,
is still life.

Love, with all its mysteries
and painful introspections,
is still love.

People, with all their flaws
and different opinions,
are still children of God.

You, with your doubts
and fears,
are still a child of God.

I, with my worries
and existential crises,
am still a child of God.

We are all children of God,
And God is love.
And God is life.

Christ-child,

Sleeping on the hay,
Swaddled safely,

Mother Mary sips some watered wine,
Offers up a thankful prayer,
Leaks a tear.

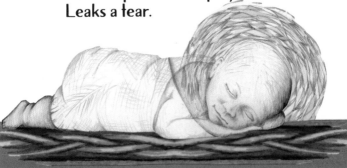

Dear God, Hold in Your arms the lost and the
lonely, the seeking and the saved.
Be gentleness to the hurting and
strength to the weary,
Give hope to the sad and forgotten,
to the despairing and the broken.
Give me the opportunity to be Your
arms and Your gentleness,
Help me to share Your hope.

I am here, in this moment,
a bringing together of all my memories,
of all my experiences,
joys, sorrows, elations, pains,
From baby to child,
teen to adult,
Your hand has held mine.
No dictator has shouted in my ear,
telling me which road to take,
Your hand has held mine
And I have just walked,
Sometimes stumbled
along the way,
Sometimes fallen
beside the way,
But Your hand has held mine,
Pulled me up and brushed me down.
Your hand has held mine.

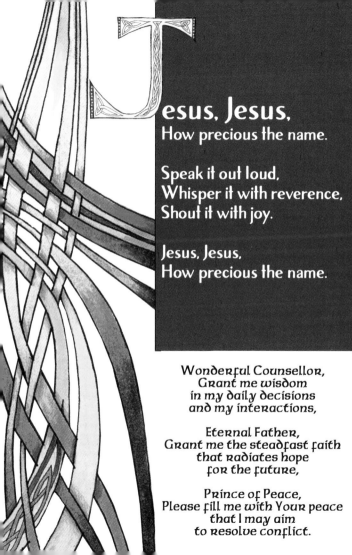

Jesus, Jesus,
How precious the name.

Speak it out loud,
Whisper it with reverence,
Shout it with joy.

Jesus, Jesus,
How precious the name.

Wonderful Counsellor,
Grant me wisdom
in my daily decisions
and my interactions,

Eternal Father,
Grant me the steadfast faith
that radiates hope
for the future,

Prince of Peace,
Please fill me with Your peace
that I may aim
to resolve conflict.

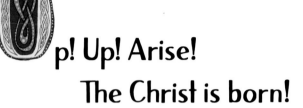

Up! Up! Arise!
The Christ is born!

In that bundled,
warm and cuddly babe
Beats the very human heart
Of the very God who created all.

Up! Up! Arise!
The Christ is born!

Bring your Gold,
Bring your incense,
Bring your precious oil.
Bring your lamb and the sauce,
Bring your sweat and toil.

Leave your pain,
Leave your sorrows,
Leave your prideful ways.
Leave your indignation,
Leave your empty days.

This baby, unconfined by time,
honour Him.
Give your self,
Give your all,
This baby, unconfined,
honour Him.

For by His Grace you are saved.

In sweet rejoicing

now sing and be glad!

Even the out-of-tune,
the sharp,
the flat,
the gasping, rasping,
crying, shouting,
the laughing, faffing,
shuffling, tapping.

Rejoice! The King is born!
Rejoice! Sing and be glad!

May my voice rise with praise to You
Uninhibited, joyful and free,
O Lord, hear my prayer!

Love was held
in the arms of love,

A Mother's fiercely protective,
gentle,
hold.

Love was held on a cross,
a sacrificial
hold.

Love holds us
in the arms of Love.

Our Creator's fiercely protective,
gentle,
hold.

Oh that this Season
would truly reflect the Glory.
Truly speak of the wonder...
God on earth...

How can we understand?
How can we see Him
through all the stuff?
How can we see Him
in the human glory and shame?

See His light in the twinkle and flash!
See His smile in the grin of a child!
See His love in the gifts exchanged!

And if He is hidden still...

Seek Him in the peaceful moments,
Seek Him in the serving of others,
Seek Him in the giving of time.

He is there.